Introduction: Voic

Poetry is, in my opinion, one of the bes thoughts, emotions, and experiences a work, can make a masterpiece.

MW01284390

The transgender community has always been fighting for a voice---for a chance to tell their stories, to educate, to have others understand. It is also easy for transgender and nonbinary individuals, especially youth, to feel alone and isolated. To be able to have access to others' stories has the potential to help a lot of people. That is why this book is currently in existence.

It started as just a dream---thoughts about how nice it would be to hear our community get a voice, to see things from different perspectives. Then I started a blog, not thinking it would lead to much. To my surprise and pleasure, more and more people started following it. People started submitting their poetry, and it was amazing to discover how happy it made them to feel as if they could be heard. I started to think my idea might not be so crazy after all.

Now, here we are. All the poems you will see in this book were submitted by young people who believed they had something to say. It may say on the cover that I am the author, but let it be known that these amazing poets were truly the ones who created this book. I made sure to show them as who they are---the genders listed alongside their names are what they identify themselves as. They deserve to have their voice, just like we all deserve to have ours.

We stand here together

Our hands linked

Our feet unsteady

All the same,

but all different

The mountains we've crossed

to get here

Left us with scars

Some say they're ugly

But we know the truth

For underneath these scars

glows the poetry on our arms

We are not our past

We are here,

now,

together.

My Gender Hurts

by Milo, 28, Genderqueer

It's so hard to nail down where you exist when you don't fit anywhere

When you float around the spectrum

Drowning in the waves

Unsure of a sense of home or a sense of belonging

Feeling the love from others but feeling so lost within yourself

The constant panic of introducing yourself or signing your name

Not knowing which one they know you by or who you should say you are

Because even you're not sure

It's impossible to try and explain it to other people

Because you're embarrassed of your identity

Of who you are

Of how you feel

Because it's such a foreign concept to live outside the lines

And heads often can't wrap around something new

Or else they just won't

I promise it confuses me more than it confuses you

Having to live in this skin that I want to simultaneously tear off and embrace

I never really fit in anyway

But this just pushes me out of "normality" even more

As if I wasn't different enough to begin with

May as well just keep the weirdo theme going

It's hard to explain

It's hard to understand

It's hard to comprehend

It's hard to exist

My gender hurts

Monsters

by Rigel, 16, Nonbinary

As a child,

You're scared of the dark.

There are monsters under the bed,

Waiting for your parents to turn off the light,

Waiting for you to hang your foot off the side of the bed,

Waiting.

And then what?

You call your parents

Ask them to check under the bed,

To check the closet,

To close the window and curtains.

To keep the monsters away.

As a teen,

You're scared of the dark,

There are monsters inside your head

Waiting for you to let down your guard

Waiting for one embarrassing moment

To ruin the rest of your night

The rest of your life.

Waiting.

So you just ride it out,

Cope the best you can,

Until you can't anymore.

You call your therapist,

Ask them for new coping mechanisms,

For new medications,

To try to hold the monsters at bay.

As a woman,

You're scared of the dark,

There are monsters everywhere.

Waiting for you to make one mistake,

To prove that your gender is inadequate.

Waiting for you to be alone,

Until you're vulnerable.

There are monsters around every corner,

Waiting for you to fail.

Waiting.

You call your best friend,

Ask her for advice,

But despite her guidance,

Nothing changes,

Nothing keeps the monsters away.

The monsters are taught

That women need to be perfect,

That women need to be more careful.

The monsters aren't taught

How to be men,

How to be civilized.

It's part of our culture that

It's easier to teach women to be perfect,

To be modest,

Than to teach men not to rape,

Not to be monsters.

As a member of the LGBT+ community

You're afraid of the dark,

Afraid of the light.

You're afraid of your own home,

Afraid of your safe spaces.

There are monsters everywhere,

Waiting for you to trip up,

To come out.

Waiting for you to want basic rights,

To exist.

Waiting.

You call your representatives,

Ask for equality,

Ask for non-discrimination laws.

Ask to be a little less scared of the dark,

But you're talking directly to the monsters,

About keeping them away.

Conditionally Out

by Clessa, 19, Genderfluid

When I told my mother I am bisexual,

She said "Okay,"

Like it was one phrase

Bridging two things she already knew.

When I told her I am genderfluid,

She said "Okay"

In a tone flat enough to drive a car across.

It sounded like "No."

It sounded like "Go to bed."

It sounded like "It's too late at night to deal with this."

When I told her I am genderfluid,

She said, "But I'm still going to call you Margaret."

It sounded like "I'm going to pretend you're not."

Too often my queerness feels like a conversation she doesn't want to have,

But I'm tired of feeling like I never came out of the closet.

She already has a son,

There is no room in this family for another man,

Another flat chest,

Another deep voice.

She didn't raise two boys,

When she had me, she prayed for a girl.

Maybe she felt like her prayers had been answered,

But God also made me who I am.

She can blame radiation,

Or pollution,

Or growth hormones in milk,

But if you are looking for somewhere to lay the blame,

Look no further than Heaven.

I was given a voice,

And you will listen to it.

Scars

by Nox, 16, Agender

I feel bad

for hating this body

because it is theoretically

beautiful

but it was carved into me

with a knife

and the scars ache

with every breath

Nesting Doll

by Kaiden, 18, Transboy

dad, I still remember the look on your face when I told you that I was transgender.

and by this I don't simply mean that I was "born in the wrong body,"

I mean that I was birthed into a mold misfigured by malevolence,

consequentially conceived in a hospital bed

and carefully constructed every day since by you,

with the sole purpose of shaping me into the perfect young woman that I am not.

I mean that when I look in the mirror I do not see myself, I see an empty shell of a body,

a desolate, detrimental and disfigured boy

who is forced to wear a dress and apply makeup.

this is not something that I made up.

I am a Russian nesting doll that does not fit into its brethren,

I am a speed limit sign for the wrong road,

I am a machine with rusted, faulty parts.

dad, you tell me to put on concealer, but it can't conceal the reality of the matter,

which is that behind your masked malice and begrudged bitterness,

you want me dead.

Boy Scouts

by Akila, 23, Transboy

Nobody knows that I don't belong.

All in Uniform they think I understand

Relate to their Lives

Even when all my Life

I was never one of them.

Nobody knows that I'm wrong.

They all think I'm shy and that's why I can't

strip off my shirt

but under my shirt

lies the truth and my shame.

Nobody knows that I don't belong.

And none of them would ever understand.

I'm not naturally afraid

just taught to be afraid,

because I am not the same.

Fluidity

by Riley, 15, Genderfluid

I wake up in the morning feeling different.

Different from the night before

Last night I felt extremely sure

That I was blue like Romeo

But now I'm reaching for my bow.

As I'm walking through the halls

Kids around me stare in awe

Though this gender I inhabit

They don't see me, only a faggot.

Today I'm not Romeo

Nor am I Juliet

Not even Benvolio

My gender is neither the set.

So I'm sitting in English class

Green bracelet on my arm

But now I feel a surge

My Stomach starts to squirm

So I reach into my bag

Adorn my band of blue

My heart rate settles down

And my joy is born anew.

Two Halves Make A Whole

by Hannah/Henry, 18, Bigender

There's girl

And then there's boy

Mutually exclusive until suddenly they're not

I look at my two halves

They've no idea what to do

Girl gets dibs cause the body fits her

But Boy wants a crack at driving too

Girl has society on her side so she near always wins

Only when Boy starts crying will she let him call the shots

Dysphoria gives him an edge

Only cause it hurts her too

They're the same person after all

I look at my two halves

They know exactly what to do

Joined together by a seam

Look each other in the eyes

Turbulent brain waves can't be sailed on

They compromise and agree

They'll take turns peacefully

Even steer together time to time

They both just want to be happy

They're not so different

They're the same person after all

And then Girl gets greedy

While Boy's tired from anxiety and corrections

Girl gets nervous

Pushes him down

Breaks the seam

She takes full command

It's easier this way

He stands out like a beacon

She can blend right in

Until Boy stands again

He wants the wheel back

The fighting starts anew

They're polar opposites once more but still the same person after all

Still the same, worn out person

Who can't understand why two halves refuse to stay whole

I Don't Belong

by Kat, 13, Genderfluid

I watch the boys run along

How I wish I could belong

But "you're a girl"

I watch the girls skip along

Every now and then I belong

Because I'm not always a girl

I watch everyone go along

Where do I belong?

I don't

I won't

Because "you're not a boy"

Because "play with girls' toys"

Because "that's not real"

Because "it doesn't matter how you feel"

Because "people that aren't cis make me want to hurl"

Because "you're a girl"

Girly Boy

by Felix, 14, Male

I am a thirteen-year-old boy with my chest wrapped in spandex

And I don't want to leave my room

Because the world is made up of sharp edges and words

And I can't help but want to cry every time I remember my average life expectancy

Twenty years

This means that I have been a teen for the past seven months and I am over middle age

Isn't that just wonderful?

Okay,

Let's talk about statistics:

87% will receive harassment at school

77% have depression and/or anxiety

50% of transgender people will be raped or sexually assaulted at some point in their life

And 41% will attempt suicide in their lives

My name is Felix and I am just a thirteen-year-old boy with my chest wrapped in spandex

And I don't want to leave my room

Because I'm scared

I Struggle To Say

by Chyler, 14, Genderfluid

Mom, I struggle to say.

They have locked me in a box, forced me to be their puppet.

They have forced me in makeup, pink dresses, bows to strangle me with.

They have forced me to grow my hair, to paint a mask onto my face.

Mom. They have locked my mind.

Kept me from learning cars and labor, freedom and truth.

They have tried to make me love a man.

They have called me young lady, girl.

Mom, please. It scares me what you would do if you knew.

What happened when your precious girl grew.

I dropped the fairy wings and found a tie.

Cut my hair and cleaned off the lies.

I bind my chest and lock my mouth.

I'm dead if the secret comes out.

I can't tell you. Dad would kill me if he knew I'm not your daughter, I might be your son.

Mom, help! You say God made me a girl for a reason.

To be objectified, insulted, sexualized?

Forced to love men and dresses?

Forced to live a lie?

Mom… I'm not sure if I am a girl.

I'd prefer not to be.

Maybe it would be better if you don't know,

You wouldn't accept me.

Dysphoria

by Kaiden, FTM

Here comes a thought, And happy doesn't describe it, But sad doesn't either.

It's the type of feeling that never leaves, The type of feeling that doesn't subside.

It feels like needles in your skin, Leaving a sting. Like hot metal dropping in cold water.

The thoughts never seem to leave. When I look in the mirror and I'm shocked By what I see, what is that supposed to mean?

When walking in the halls I feel like two people: My soul and my body. Why do I feel like this?

It affects my mood, My sleep, my appetite. All thoughts piling up in my head like paperwork Causing all the others to instantly vanish.

I walk through life as two people: What everyone sees and who I really am. One day the two will merge but the question is:

Would everyone accept it that way?

There goes thought. It might alarm you but I'm fine, I just need time to think.

I just need time to get lost in thought.

I Am From

by Katie, 17, Demigirl

I am from here,

The present,

This earth

This one tiny yet somehow

Infinitely large yet somehow

Finite universe,

I am from a world built with bricks,

And brought to life by "Logos"

The act of giving something a name

And that act allowing the breath of life to seep into that something,

That is still yet unknown,

I am from a world ripped apart by war,

As I float away into the darkness

And sit on my measly little chunk of rock and watch

As my life disappears,

I am from a world where I don't exist,

I am from a world where I took the road less traveled,

I am from a world where, and I quote:

"I take the light wonder bombs to the point in the universe where sound does end

It's the back porch of God's summer home and it's so peaceful there

You float

And it feels the way cotton candy tastes",

But I am also from a world where I have died,

A world where bleak dullness is normal,

Where life only exists to end,

A world colored burgundy-red by blood spilt from the wrist

I am from a world where my best friend has died 17 times in a row

Today,

And a world where I miss them.

Even though they're right next to me,

I am from this world,

And that world,

And all the worlds trapped between the spaces,

All the worlds trapped between the moments,

Where are you from?

House but not a Home

by Sebastian, 16, Male

I live in a house

It's not my home

Go into the attic

all the boxes filled with sadness

Go into my room

Find sleepless nights

Upstairs

Complete hate

Downstairs

Loathing

This house is not my home

This house is my body

My body is not mine

I am not home in my body

Why?

My mind

Male

My body

Female

Definition

by Faith/Coco, 19, Agender

In a world

Where words are spewed every day

It is easy to be pulled and whirled

Dazed in the confusion, lose your way.

In this hazy cloud

It can be hard to define yourself

The world is overbearing and loud

But I choose to assert myself.

I am not bound to how the world sees my face

I used to live like that, trapped in false reflections

Caught in the world, convinced I was a head case

Beaten down with false hopes and rejections.

It took a long time to see

For my wings to grow

To set me free

And for me to know.

I am my own

Strong and wondering

But I'm still becoming more because I'm not yet fully grown

I must go on, my strength thundering.

This world doesn't define me

I choose my definition

Clear the clouds and I'm truly free

No longer trapped in submission.

So you ask me who I am

I cannot give you just one word

One word can't make you give a damn

One term to define me would just be absurd.

I'm not limited to a page

It can't hold my true meaning

Life is a stage

And I will perform beaming.

One word is never enough.

Thoughts

by Drew, 21, Agender

I don't want to be a statistic

But I am

I don't want these mental illnesses

But I have them

I don't want to need special circumstances

But I do

I want a family; parents and siblings

But I don't have those

I want a home

But I don't have one

I want to be healthy

But I'm not

I need support

And I have it

I need hope for the future

And I'm working on it

I need to know that I am not a waste

And I will

My Mother's Tears

by Mason, 17, Nonbinary trans boy

When I was a little girl, life was but a perfect mirage

Now I must try to maintain a porcelain façade.

I wish I could wipe away my mother's tears

But I'm too busy cowering from my fears.

When I first told her I liked girls I was met with disbelief

Yet I got acceptance years later to my relief.

Now that I know I'm a boy, do I want to give her that grief?

I wish I could wipe away my mother's tears.

I want to leave it all behind.

I wish there was a way to hit rewind

Or conquer the demons of my mind

But I'm too busy cowering from my fears.

Maybe one day my horizons will be wide

Where I can express my pride.

I wish I could wipe away my mother's tears

But I'm too busy cowering from my fears.

Genderfluid

by Spencer, 18, Genderfluid

Dressing and undressing in the dark

(My body, my clothes are at fault)

I always avoid the gaze of the mirror

(But it feels so heavy on my back)

I want to change the way you see me

(My name, the way you address me)

But a mean voice tells me this isn't right

(And I'm so scared of being bullied)

I dream of missing things I'd like to add

(If only for a day)

I dream of removing things I don't like

(If only for a day)

And when I wake up I scream and cry

(I am a monster)

Because I've changed again overnight

(And I wasn't born how I'd have liked)

A dress, pants, it doesn't look right

(Will it ever feel like it's fitting?)

My hair is too long, too short

(I've tried a thousand hairstyles)

Keeping my hairy legs seems okay

(But then again, sometimes it isn't)

I fear the gaze of other people

(But it's mine who's the scariest)

My gender is fluid

(That means it changes)

For you it could be a dream

(But for me it's reality)

Please, take me seriously

(That's all I ask)

A little bit of encouragement

(And once in a while a smile)

Wild Rose

by Spencer, 18, Genderfluid

You guessed I was a play-along girl

A happy-go-lucky with pink lips girl

A tender marshmallow perched on high heels

You thought I'd have to be a quiet listen-and-agree girl

A don't-look-further-than-the end-of-my-pretty-nose girl

Because your open eyes don't see what I've been concealing

Yeah, you didn't grasp the whole picture

You didn't walk through the door to my core

Oh, I'm a wild rose with petals dressed for a funeral

My roots run from the ground to the sky

And I sharpen my thorns every time I go out

Oh, when I open my bitter mouth

You either get the ocean on a stormy day

Or a water drop, no in between

Oh, I suffocate in the daylight

And I drown in the night's darkness

So I hide in my room and burn scented candles

I know very well what you're doing

And I will never allow you to

Cause I've got my dignity, you know

And it makes me sad you want to hurt me

Cause even if I'm strong, I'm weak too

You're wasting your time by trying to define me

One day you'll see how much wrong you did me

And that day you'll realize you hurt yourself too

Oh, I'm a wild rose with petals dressed for a funeral

My roots run from the ground to the sky

And I sharpen my thorns every time I go out

Oh, when I open my bitter mouth

You either get the ocean on a stormy day

Or a water drop, no in between

Oh, I suffocate in the daylight

And I drown in the night's darkness

So I hide in my room and burn scented candles

Call Me They

by Kat, 13, Nonbinary

I know that I seemed like a girl

I still do

I like skirts and heels

I paint my nails and wear makeup

I love the color pink

It never made you think

No, I couldn't be anything other than a girl

I would give myself curls

My lips were pink, my cheeks were red

But my breasts made me wish I was dead

You called me "she"

I wanted "they"

I've kept that secret to this day

I wear skirts and paint my nails

But you calling me my birth name is getting stale

I'm trapped in this body

I try to claw my way out

No matter how hard I try

You'll never doubt

That I'm your perfect daughter, your kind sister, your wonderful girlfriend

I have many mental wounds to mend

But I'll be okay

I'll live another day

It just makes me stronger

I can live a little longer

Because someday

You'll call me "they"

Something You Will Never Understand

by Lee, 21, Nonbinary

I am not going to divulge my pain to you.

My pain is always on display. And at first I

was happy to oblige. I'd spent 18 years in a wrought iron shoebox.

The kind you'd bury a rat in.

Stuffing fear into my mouth to keep from drawing blood.

Looping honeysuckle through my fingers to keep

from scratching my skin off.

Ask me about my pain! My blinding rage!

My denial of biblical proportions! HELL!

When I am alone I dip my hands into the water and

feel very small again. Like I could feign sleep and he

would carry me to bed.

I can't get out of bed. I am everything all the time.

A sucking chest wound with pronouns.

I am not going to divulge my pain to you.

I couldn't hide it if I tried, I am corroded, my mouth

Still tastes rivers of politicized iron on the locker room floor.

I want to be the sword.

I am only my hands in the water, pushing against the current.

My "Little" Monster

by Cass, 19, Genderflux

Everyone has

Their flaws

Their imperfections

Their monsters.

No matter who you are

Small monsters

Large monsters

Many or few monsters.

But there are a few

Who would not be accepted

Who are not accepted

Because of their "Little" Monsters.

They cover it up

They hide it away

They deeply believe

They cannot be accepted.

These few hide among us

They are like everyone else

They are only loved when they cover up

Their horrible "Little" Monsters.

The minority who allow
Their monsters out of the cage
Are rarely loved
More often they are cast away.

I was among these few
I let my "Little" Monster out
And was cast aside
Thrown out
As if I
Were no more
Than trash.

I tried to push my "Little" Monster away
I tried to make them forget
But they wouldn't
They couldn't
They would always
Remember.

And so I left that prison of hate
And went somewhere new
And made sure to never let my "Little" Monster out.

But slowly
I can sense it creeping out

It's crawling out of its cage

Desperate for the light of day.

And

I'm not

Cast away.

Identity

by Ronnie, 19, Nonbinary

Who am I?

I keep asking myself this question

Never quite finding the right answer

I know this much at least

I'm not your little girl

The things you call me are falling apart at the seams

And I'm left standing here

Not nameless, just unsure

Creating a name of my own

The world is not black and white

I wish I could tell you

Maybe you'd get it

But how do I explain what I feel when I don't understand it myself?

Oh, but why should it matter?

I love myself whether you do or don't

So treat me as you will

Call me whatever you wish

I am not what you think I am

I am more than how you perceive me

I am not what you wanted me to be

Nor what I thought I was

I am so much more

And less and not at all

I'm everchanging

Which face should I wear tonight?

Make Believe

by Ashton, 18, Bigender

When you're told every day

That it's in your head

That it doesn't exist

That it's just a phase

That you're just confused

That no one cares

You begin to believe it

Until the person you thought you were

Is Stripped

Torn

Taken

Make-believed away

And all that's left is this person;

You don't recognize them

Their fake smile

Their empty eyes

Their illegitimate tears

Because finally, they're what everybody thought you were

But you.

There Are No Princesses Here

by Charlie, 17, Trans boy

You left me behind at age seven,

but now, I'm on your head again.

Your thick dirty blonde curls look

like Courtney Love's- oh how you tried

for hours to get your hair like hers,

even though, I know you want

hair like her husband's instead.

But, how sweet it is; if I had eyes,

I would cry rhinestone tears of joy

for you. You're growing up, and

my thick plastic is too thick a barrier now.

My bright bismuth coloration is

childish and flashy, and you are neither;

my combs no longer secure me to you,

but they dig into your scalp-

your head is bigger than I remember,

but I suppose it has been nine years

since you last placed me on my perch, and

somehow the pressure of me feels as though

you are trying to squeeze yourself into a

pearl- you wear enough black to be coal, but

it pains me because you think you are

Santa's scraps for naughty children, and

you are trying too hard to be the pretty pearl

that they push you to be; I know you have rules.

Wear pretty princess dresses that compress

Depress, but giggle like a bell, speak in soprano

Like you did when you were nine, and

when your hair was white blonde, eyes cerulean

and wide- wide as your gap-toothed smile-

Stop Growing Up, they say, they beg, but

I know. I know you can't let that happen.

That's not how it's supposed to be.

You are caught between obedience and flying.

You are supposed to see the world expand,

You have to meet Sally with pigtails at age twenty

And you have to meet Bob, who

Majors in science and fashion, like an enigma

You are supposed to see Jane who changed her name

because Jonathan just didn't fit;

you are supposed to relate to her change,

because you are making one that is so very similar,

and you are supposed to laugh with Alex,

who is funny through every hardship that hurts them,

and you need to see Darcy, whose eyes crinkle when she grins.

You are supposed to see everything great and magical,

everything that will make you cry and ache;

you are supposed to feel like you could save the world,

and you are supposed to realize that

even if you can only save one person, it's okay for that

person to be yourself; you have to learn how to break

and how to put yourself back together.

I will move on to other heads of silk and curl and art.

I will miss you, but I know that one day,

when you put me down, it will be the last time

you've ever picked me up; the last time I take my perch,

and perhaps it is today. Your sweet sixteen is almost over,

you know. I will miss your Courtney Love, rose hairspray curls.

And you won't miss me because I am something juvenile;

I am something fantastical; I am something unreal

I am something fake; I am something plastic; I am a toy.

I am fit for a princess, but

There are no princesses here.

There are no queens, either.

You know what you are.

You are a king,

and kings don't wear tiaras.

I can't wait to watch you wear your crown.

Not Included

by Aiden, 17, Nonbinary

I sometimes wonder

What you really think

Of me

You say you love me

And respect me for who I am

But I can't help but wonder

If you lie

To spare me of my feelings

Because you wish

For me to be a girl

For me to wear dresses

And makeup

Because when you say

You're a lesbian

And that girls are so beautiful

I know

That I'm not included

Or, in your mind

Maybe I am

The Mask

by Blue, 15, Nonbinary

I see the light every morning

"Ugh, here we go again."

Getting ready to go to school

"Oh wait, I forgot my mask."

I pick up the round, flat object

Painted white with a smile

Showing a girl who loves herself

And is doing okay and is nice

I have had this mask my whole life

Before I go, I look in the mirror

And see my own face

It shows the actual me

A tired person who is done with life

They are closeted and it's running them down

And friends depression and anxiety are here too

They help me put the mask on

"Alright, let's go."

Brotherhood

by Bane, 19, Trans guy

broth·er·hood 'brəT Hər,ho od/ noun

1. Our fathers never taught us to play rough. We grew up in dresses that were tight in all the wrong places and makeup that sat heavy in the summer. Our mothers yelled at us for coming home, mud-covered and sun stricken. Red cheeks from the heat instead of the blush. We learned to apply ourselves to actions before we learned the power of words

2. It's winter and we always loved how the coats hid our chest. We sat in the back of the schoolyard and smoked because nobody could tell what was our breath and what wasn't and we compared the freckles on our arms. We clicked our shoes on the pavement and talked about "the sun is so warm even though it's so cold" and "look how sharp my jaw looks today" and "I was called 'sir' last night and something in my chest tried to fly" and "do you think my mother would still love me if she knew"

3. I learned quickly that secrets are kept between friends. That there's a bond you create over secrecy and self-doubt and discovery that few can break

4. I never had a brother, but I always knew I was meant to be a man

Burnt Skin

by Orion, 18, Trans boy

The sleeves of my shirt are soft under my fingers

As I tug on them in a nervous fidget

While struggling to meet the eyes watching me

They can't see what's inside of me

But they judge every single movement I make

Deciding if I'm this or that without hearing my voice

They don't care about the stories that I have built

Inside of my mind

For centuries

What matters to them is how I present

What my body looks like

And how their rules can be applied, making me smaller

I am not their idea of perfection and I will never fit the cast they used to produce the perfect army

Because while their creations are seeds buried deep underground

I am a spirit painting the sky with my mind

Though they don't understand what I say

And their eyes burn holes on my skin

I won't ever abandon who I am

My Gender Is Up Here

by Benjamin, 16, Trans man

'Are you a boy or a girl?'

They shout down the corridor in a chorus behind me

Like the cries of "Good morning, Miss" in assembly

The patronizing tone

in sleep-deprived confusion

Droning throughout the halls

ringing around 'she'.

Going to lessons is the scariest thing

Head down, walking fast hoping

they'll never say anything

Hoping no one will question you

Glance around and notice you

not daring to look up

in case you make a wrong move

You can't know what it's like to be

In a room all alone

In a house that is not your own

'Your body is a temple' they said

But they don't tell you how to treat it

if it's right in your head

but wrong in your skin

and that feeling

of being and existing

is like dealing

with a thousand anxieties

suffocating within;

Chest too obvious

voice too loud and feminine

not enough to be 'gentleman'.

'Why does this bother you?'

I hear you inquire

It's because society's construct

of gender is too based on attire;

an old-fashioned concept-

Telling your children

That 'blue's for boys'

'Pink's for girls'.

'Is it really?' I say

Gender is not just binary

it fluxes and changes,

just like any scientific theory

Einstein for instance,

didn't come up with special relativity

in a night

It took years of work

until he was right

Let this apply for gender too:

not just black

and white it's not as

clear cut as that;

Evolve the theory

from system to spectrum

of freedom and pride

to reside in one's body happily:

Humanity allied.

This is what I dream about,

But this is not what

I've been living throughout

In our world of shame;

where we are reduced to words and themes.

Driving my community,

those who love and support me,

to thoughts of suicide-

being known

only when they're reduced

to rags and bones

dead bodies

hanging

from their hashtags,

thrown in the corner,

another into the pile of disorder.

But people think it's okay

To come up to you and

abuse you in the street

Knocked to your knees

to cries of 'queer'

You end up living in fear-

what do you expect given

who's watching Wall Street?

Yet I stand here

Talking to you

A queer boy-

With all connotations of the word-

A queer boy with a voice.

Look at me!

My chest,

My unbroken voice,

My broken mind,

I am not proud of what I am-

What I've become-

How much it hurts

Is indescribable.

I am not what you want me to be

I am a man

Not trans.

Made in the USA
Monee, IL
24 March 2022

93501741R00031